CW00924266

Confident Parenting

Restoring your confidence as a parent by making yourself the project and not trying to change your child

Dr Jenny Brown

*This book is partly based on a chapter in Jenny Brown's book: "Growing Yourself Up: How to bring your best to all of life's relationships [Exisle Publishing, 2017]; Chapter 8: Grown-up parenting. It includes additional resources from Jenny's manualised program: The Parent Hope Project: www.parenthopeproject.com.au

Disclaimer

While this book is intended as a general information resource and all care has been taken in compiling the contents, this book does not take account of individual circumstances and is not in any way a substitute for professional advice. Always consult a qualified practitioner or therapist. Neither the author nor the publisher and their distributors can be held responsible for any loss, claim or action that may arise from reliance on the information contained in this book.

Dr Jenny Brown is passionate about helping parents to bring their best to this vital role in life. Hence, she has developed "The Parent Project" a resources web site, to assist parents to regain their compass as loving leaders for their children. Jenny has been working in the field of child and family mental health and family therapy since the 1980s; and has trained professionals in the field for over 3 decades. Her Ph.D. research was exploring parents' experience of their child's mental health treatment. A key finding was that: "When parents shifted from being invested in external 'expert' treatment to having a sense of their capacities to make a difference for their child, they finished the [treatment] program with increased hope." Jenny is a writer and speaker on family and parenting matters. Amongst several publications, she is the author of the best-selling book: 'Growing Yourself Up: How to bring your best to all of life's relationships.'

Jenny founded the Family Systems Institute, Sydney Australia in 2004. She is a clinical member and supervisor for the Australian Association of Family Therapy. In 2018 she received the ANJFT award for distinguished contribution to family therapy in Australia. Her academic training has been at the University of Sydney, Columbia University New York, and the University of New South Wales. Additionally, Jenny has completed in-depth training in family therapy & family systems at Relationships Australia, The Family Institute of Westchester New York, & the Tavistock and Portman Trust, London.

Jenny's most important credential is as a parent of adult children and a proud grandparent.

Contents

Introduction

Confident Parenting: The Parent is the project not the child

Extra Resources for Building Confident Parents

References

Further resources

Confident Parenting

Introduction

If you are reading this little book you clearly want to be the best resource possible for your children's growth in resilience and maturity. Most parents want this. They are conscientious and try to learn about their child's needs at various stages of children's development. However, this mini book is not focused on understanding your child. Instead, it is based on research findings that reveal that the more a parent focuses on trying to understand and influence their child, the less confident they are about themselves as a parent leader. A well-intentioned focus on helping a child can easily lead to a confused and intense parent-child relationship where the child in fact becomes reactive to their parent's monitoring. When a child becomes our project, even when we are motivated by love and care, the child may lose the necessary emotional space for them to gradually grow into responsibly independent young people. This is how I have described this predicament: "An intense child focus, which can be positive or negative, presents significant developmental challenges to the young person as they come to function in reaction to others. This leaves them with little emotional breathing space to grow in thinking, feeling and acting for themselves." (J. Brown, 2008). So, what does a parent do with their strong instinct to care for and protect their child? This is not a simple question! A first step is to get a focus back on being a thoughtful observer of how you relate to your children (as distinct from an observer of your children). What is the effect of your responses to your children? What is the 'big picture' goal of your parenting? Perhaps the most important question is: Can I parent calmly or does worry create an unhelpful intensity to some of my parenting responses? Does one of my children particularly push my worry triggers, and does this shape me to be a different kind of parent for that child?

The reading that follows is partly an edited excerpt from a bigger book about maturity in relationships: Growing Yourself Up: How to bring your best to all of life's relationships (J. Brown, Exisle Publishers, 2017). The details for accessing this book can be found at the end of this book. The resources sections come from my manualised Parent programs - The Parent Hope and Parent Confidence Project. While I write from my own experiences of clinical practice, teaching, research, and my family life, the core ideas in this little book come from the ground-breaking research and theory of Dr Murray Bowen. Bowen was a prominent psychiatrist and research scientist from the 1950s to his death in 1990. His 'family systems theory' is a gift for making sense of ourselves in our important relationships. It shows us predicable ways that tension fuels ways of relating to other family members. We are so much more than a bunch of separate individuals in our families; we are part of a collection of people who form a system.

In our family system we are always affecting each other in ways we usually don't realise. Family members' sensitivities to each other are always flowing back and forth, and shaping us differently. This means that it only takes one person in a family to manage themselves in a more thoughtful and calm manner and the benefits can ripple out to each person.

My hope is that the ideas and examples that follow will help to restore your confidence as a parent and enable you to make yourself the project as a way of loving your children.

Jenny Brown PhD

Note: At the end of the book you will find some links to further resources to build your parenting confidence. Many such resources can be found on my web site: www.parentproject. com.au

Confident Parenting

The Parent is the project not the child

'Parents are the hope of civilization. Much depends on whether parents can connect in a meaningful, positive way with each other and with their children. If they can, a generation may emerge ready to tackle and reverse some ominous trends.'

—Roberta Gilbert MD

Today's parenting: swimming in a sea of anxiety

The task of being a confident parent is perhaps more difficult to achieve than ever. In our current anxious, child-focused society it requires a parent to swim against the emotional tide. We will need to shift our focus away from doing for and worrying about our child and back to being a responsible self. Around my neighbourhood the worst of the morning peak hour is at school drop-off time. Frazzled parents are chauffeuring their children to school with minutes to spare before class begins. They are checking to see that their child has all their homework and correct books for the day's lessons. Children are delivered to the school gate carrying gym bags, musical instruments and laptops for extracurricular activities. The sight of groups of children walking or riding bikes to school has become a novelty. What is going on here?

It seems that the more frantic the pace of life becomes, and the more anxiety mounts about our uncertain future, the more society panders to its children. There is less space for children to think and solve problems for themselves, as both parents and schools manage their schedules for them. While the statistics tell us that those who abuse children are usually within the family or known by the family, the anxiety about 'stranger danger' and the risks of leaving a child unaccompanied by an adult have contributed to the demise of children finding their own way to school. Parents are increasingly taking over their children's homework assignments so that they don't fall behind in an increasingly results-driven climate. When a child stumbles at school, parents move in to complain to the school about not protecting their child. The school recommends a range of professional interventions to prevent the child from struggling. Meanwhile many children are less able to take a stand for themselves against schoolyard teasing; they are less able to direct their own learning efforts; and when adolescence arrives, they are ill prepared for managing their new freedoms responsibly.

The sea of ever-changing advice coming from child psychology has not always helped parents who want to do their best for their child. Peter Stearns, a professor of social history at George Mason University, Washington DC, has studied trends in US parenting over the last century. He notes that as parenting manuals emerged in the twentieth century they became a stimulus and outlet for parents' worries and added fuel to a 'century of anxiety about the child and about parents' own adequacy'. As parents outsource their development of child-rearing wisdom they can easily become more uncertain in themselves.

Can you see the parenting challenge in the midst of this rush to take over children's capacities to soothe their upsets and solve their problems? If you're going to assist your child to grow their resilience, the first step will be to increase your own resilience in tolerating your child's upset without feeling compelled to rush in and smooth over everything for them. The grown-up parent, who really wants to be a loving resource to their child, is prepared to work on themselves and not make a project out of their child.

Helping children through your own maturity
Ed and Linda relished the prospect of starting a family as soon as they had established some degree of financial security. For many of their early years of marriage they enjoyed imagining the large family they would have. They spoke of how their children would enjoy the huge stores of affection that both felt they had to give.

Linda viewed her own parents as cold and distant. She was the eldest of two daughters and was distressed to recall the struggles her younger sister Rebecca experienced with depression and school difficulties. Her mother, with her dad's support, had channelled much of her energy into getting help for Rebecca. Despite her parents' efforts, Linda believed that the lack of affection in her family was to blame for her sister's struggles. She was determined to reverse this in her own family by being always available to her children and showering them with praise and warmth.

Ed was supportive of this approach. He had come from a family where his father used alcohol to switch off after work and the rest of the family walked on eggshells around him, trying to avoid an angry outburst. Ed was pleased to have found a woman like Linda who was going to be such a good mother. He was anxious about his fathering and was secure in the belief that Linda was going to lead the way in creating the happy family they both dreamed of.

After giving birth to three children within five years, Linda and Ed were feeling exhausted from chronic sleep deprivation and the energy being invested in their children. Ed was showing signs of severe burnout and was fearful that he could no longer maintain proficiency in his job as a teacher. Linda was supportive of his efforts to get some help for his symptoms so that they could keep things afloat.

It was at this point that I came to hear of this family's story. Ed came to counselling wanting to address his levels of anxiety and exhaustion. I recall him saying, 'I have only ever wanted to be a good father and a good provider; but the way I'm feeling lately I am not much use to anyone. I actually would just like to be able to run off to a retreat somewhere and not be responsible for anything.'

As Ed reflected on his fathering, he could see that he was consumed with affirming his children and guiding them well.

He was crushed by his growing impatience with his eldest child. He feared that he was becoming an angry, disengaged parent just like his experience of his own father. He and Linda had read just about every parenting book available but were finding that the more they read the more confused they were becoming. They found themselves trying all manner of techniques to manage the increasingly anxious behaviour of Harry, their seven-year-old son, and their five-year-old daughter Shari's defiance. In any one day Ed found himself using time out, spanking, removal of TV, lying down with his kids to help them sleep and giving sticker rewards for good behaviour. The anxieties of their eldest son Harry had started to emerge at school and the teachers were concerned about his slow progress with reading. Ed felt that Harry was frightened to make any mistakes at school.

When I met with Ed and Linda together I heard that she also was feeling overwhelmed and directionless as a parent. Linda said, 'I have worked so hard to be up on all the latest parenting techniques and child development knowledge. You can't imagine how deflated I am that two of my children are not settled and happy.'

Overly focusing on having happy children

In turning to outside professional sources, Linda and Ed were desperate to be perfect parents for their children. The problem with this emphasis on what the books and courses said should happen was that Linda and Ed were borrowing their wisdom from others. In the process they stopped developing their inner adult, who thinks through dilemmas for themselves before rushing to get an expert's opinion. The other problem of focusing on the 'how to' of parenting, is losing a focus on growing oneself. Mature parenting is not related to good technique but to nurturing a parent's character. I remember Ed's comments when he started to realise this: 'Wow, I'd not really ever stopped to notice how much of my energy has been going into trying to have healthy and happy children. I haven't given myself much of a look-in. I guess it's not any wonder that I've fallen in such a heap.'

Ed began to see that in trying to get his children to be a certain way, he was neglecting clarifying and managing how he wanted to be as a husband and father. In beginning to redirect his focus away from the children and onto his management of himself, Ed began to pay attention to how often he tried to push, pull or praise his children. He practised pulling back and thinking through how he could manage his own emotions and then to let his children know what he stood for. This meant he got clearer about what he was willing to do for his kids and what he expected them to learn to do for themselves. As with any growing-up effort, the valuable progress comes gradually but Ed could quite quickly see the benefits of turning his attention from his children to managing himself better.

Linda was also encouraged by Ed's improved clarity and started to get interested in re-focusing her worries from her children to herself. As a result, they both started to talk more to each other about themselves, their experiences, their challenges and what they were each encouraged by in all parts of their life. As a couple they began to talk less about how to help the children and more about their values as parents and what kind of balance each wanted to get back into their lives. They also started to be more of a fun couple again. Their sense of humour seemed to have been left behind at the very thought of pregnancy.

Being clearer about expectations

Ed reported on the growing-up progress he was making, giving an example of how he managed himself at a recent school meeting about Harry. He and Linda were meeting with Harry's teacher about her concerns that he might have a learning delay. Ed reflected:

> I was able to listen to the teacher's concerns and ask her questions. But for the first time, I was able to think for myself about Harry and give my different point of view. I said that I would be okay about reviewing things at the end of the year, but I saw that a big part of Harry's problems were tied up in him being too anxious about everyone's expectations. I really stood by my new commitment to taking all this pressure off Harry.

Ed went on to say that when the teacher suggested an intensive reading course for Harry, he was clear in expressing his newly clarified view that what Harry needed most was to have some more breathing space to find his own learning potential. Linda was less certain about this approach but willing to give it a go. The teacher said she was concerned but would be happy to see how things went over the next term.

Ed's changed interactions went like this:

Harry: 'Dad, I can't do this reading! Can you come and read me a story?'

Ed: 'Harry, I am not going to come to your room until I've

finished helping Mum clean up. When I come I am willing to share the reading of your school book that you've been working on.'

Harry starts whinging: 'Mum, Dad won't read me a story. Dad, you are being mean!'

Ed replies calmly and firmly: 'I have nothing more to say, Harry. I'll be in to join in your reading when I'm ready.'

Ed and Linda did not respond to Harry's protests. When Ed went to his son's bedroom at his usual time, he said: 'Show me where you're up to Harry and I will read the next three pages with you, taking it in turns.'

Ed didn't check up on how much practice Harry had done, he simply joined in reading a paragraph at a time. He didn't over-praise Harry's efforts but asked him what he liked about the story and to share his favourite character.

Ed was really motivated to change his old ways of behaving. This came from his clarity that his old approach wasn't working for his child or for his functioning as a healthy adult in the world. He determined to stop looking to the latest parenting fad for advice and began to turn his attention to his own self-management. He also began to work on bridging the distant relationship he had with his ageing parents and getting out more just with Linda. Ed also knew he would have to tolerate Harry's clinging and that his apparently helpless behaviour may continue to invite him back into doing too much for him again. He had seen enough early encouraging signs that, when left to his own devices, Harry could achieve more than he had imagined was possible.

Grown-up parents help grow up children

I can relate to the path on which Ed and Linda found themselves. When I first became a parent I recall feeling enormous pressure to get it right and not damage my children. I also felt niggling uncertainties about whether I was up to this job. Many parents, to varying degrees, struggle to get balanced about the amount of attention they give their children. With all the best intentions, we conscientious parents have a tendency to shift our focus from our own responsibilities to attending to our children's happiness.

Here's a nutshell description of what can happen with an increase in worry focus directed towards a child. See if you can follow this common cycle for conscientious, caring parents:

» In response to a parent's concerned attentions, the child becomes attuned to being nervously monitored and reacts with increasing self-consciousness.

» The child's anxious response can be in the form of increased neediness or agitated behaviour. An aroused child usually increases their impulsive and demanding behaviour, while a needy child increases their dependence.

» The parents, in turn, may inadvertently increase their focus on fixing things for the child by either increasing their corrections or their support. In this concern-driven cycle, the parent partly gives up being a separate person from the child and the child grows up borrowing some of their self from the reactions they elicit from their parent.

» The aroused child is restricted in their capacity to find ways to calm themself and contain their impulsiveness; and the needy child is compromised in learning to manage their own worries.

When a child's behaviour is anxious or unsettled it gets tricky to see the bigger picture of the parent–child circular dance. It's all too easy to think that the problem is in the child who is, after all, showing symptoms. On the other hand, the parent can be blamed for being too lenient or too harsh. What is harder to see is that the problem is mostly being generated by the reactions between people, not simply from within one individual. Both parents and children are triggering certain behaviours in the other. For example, when a child is whinging and clingy, it's all too easy to see the problem residing in the individual rather than in the system of interactions. The grown-up challenge is for the parent to look at how their efforts to assist the child may be stirring up an increase in the child's anxiety-driven reactions.

When parents start getting over-involved in either negative or positive ways with their children, this is often an overflow of tension from another relationship. Tensions that have not been figured out with parents or spouses get so easily redirected into trying to make everything work for the next generation. In the process we adults stop being direct with each other about our own concerns and insecurities and one of our children can step into the connection gaps that have been unknowingly left open for them.

Reactions to the other parent

When a child is struggling in any way it is predictable that each parent becomes increasingly sensitive to the way the other parent is interacting with the child. It is all too easy to find fault in the other parent and to begin to parent more in reaction to them than in a thoughtful stance with our child. Parents begin to interfere with each other, to critique the other, or try to compensate for what we think is wrong with our spouse's parenting. This adds to confusion for children who start to align with the parent who advocates for a softer approach and distance from the parent who is reactively trying to be the 'firm' one. Such a triangle is remarkably common in families, with the parent who feels like an outsider becoming quite resistant to any of their spouse's efforts to change them. Each parent would do well to stop trying to change their spouse or their child and instead invest their efforts into constructively adjusting themselves.

Children so easily fill a breach in their parents' marriage. The solution is to be found in one or both parents shifting their focus off their child, away from the other parent and back onto their own issues and responsibilities. Responsible, mature parents, with clear inner convictions, will in turn allow more scope for the development of responsible self-directed children.

A healthy connection with your children

You may be thinking that all this emphasis on getting the focus away from our children and back onto our own responsibilities ignores the important relationship bond that is required for a child to grow up securely. Attachment between parent and child is wired into our biology and even begins in the uterus as a foetus is able to discriminate its mother's voice from the voices of others. The challenge of healthy attachment with our children is to keep our attentiveness in proportion. The worst forms of neglect and rejection of children grow out of an idealised parent–child bond where the first signs of lack of compliance by the child are experienced by the parent as an intolerable threat to the perfect harmony they imagined. An over-idealised bond with a child can conversely take the form of too much smothering, where the child is slowed from developing as a separate person.

The following list compares the qualities of a *healthy, mature* connection with your children with an *out-of-proportion connection*, which in Bowen's theory is also referred to as fusion.

Healthy, mature connection

When part of a healthy and mature connection with our children, each person:

» enjoys both time together and time apart;

» treats each other with warmth and respect;

» displays acts of kindness and affection;

» tolerates the other being upset with them;

» is able to have disagreements without breaking the relationship;

» takes responsibility for their actions;

» responds thoughtfully.

Out-of-proportion connection

Conversely, in an exaggerated connection, or fusion, each person may:

» feel uncomfortable with separation;

» need the other to be happy with them all the time;

» expect the other to make them feel good;

» stay silent on their view because of fear of conflict;

» mind-read or speak for the other;

» think more about the relationship than their own responsibilities;

» respond anxiously.

The shift from a stifling connection to a balanced connection can bring marked changes to the parent–child relationship — indeed to all relationships. A mother of a fifteen-year-old recently described this change:

> Before I started to work on my own limits with Sophie, she was shifting from awful defiance to childlike clinging to me. She was escaping out of her bedroom window most nights to hang out with friends and the next minute she'd be sitting on top of me wanting me to hug her like a baby. This was really doing my head in with her both rebelling and clinging like crazy. But over the past few months, as I have become a clearer parent, she's treating me with more respect. I'm no longer stopping what I'm doing to give her a hug but we are going for coffee together and she's talking more than I can remember. I cancelled her mobile phone connection last week and she stopped talking to me for a couple of days, but yesterday she was telling me all about her textile assignment and asking me about my day. I can actually see that we could become friends as the adult years get closer.

How parenting revealed my own immaturity
After four years of marriage, my husband David and I

excitedly welcomed our first child, Jacqueline. She was the first grandchild, which meant a significant new chapter for every member of the extended family. It is not surprising that Jacqueline, like other eldest children and first grandchildren, has grown up under a spotlight. It's not easy for such children to learn to tolerate being part of a crowd without standing out.

We doted on our daughter and relished the attention she received from the wider family. As Jacqueline showed signs of evening colic, I struggled to settle her to sleep at night and became anxious about the detrimental effect of a baby crying for extended periods with her parents unable to soothe her. Like many first-time parents, I feared that she might be somehow scarred for life.

I admit I was completely unprepared for the extent of the changes that came with becoming a parent. My marriage had felt solid during the pregnancy but the job of raising a child meant lots of new things had to be negotiated. How were we going to share the load of caring for our child, dealing with domestic order and a change in our financial circumstances? No advice could adequately have prepared me for the sleep deprivation and increase in demands that I felt. Time to just chill out as a married couple had been suctioned away by the intensity of our new roles.

Rather than recognise and soothe my own anxieties about my transition to parenting, I readily focused on Jacqueline. This detouring of my uncertainties meant that I became sensitive to any sign of insecurity in Jacqueline. I responded with doting attention and stimulation. Not surprisingly, Jacqueline did develop quite distressing tantrums around age three and displayed significant jealousy of her sister Katie when she was born. This was demonstrated through aggressive behaviour such as pushing her baby sister's head into the ground and an episode of using her new safety scissors to give her sister a 'back to the scalp' haircut. While the punk hairstyle episode is retold two decades later with much humour, I can now look back and understand that it was more than quaint playfulness. My intense investment in my first child was not helping her to be able to tolerate sharing my attention with her sister.

David and I stumbled our way through the maze of early family life with times of joyfulness intertwined with chaos. My focus on giving our children the attention I thought they required, and seeking to meet what I perceived to be the expectations of doting grandparents, meant that my 'inner adult' got a bit lost. In order to grow up in this stage of my life I needed to step back from the focus on keeping children and extended family pleased in order to get my individual act together.

Rewards and punishments: lessons from puppy management
Whenever I present a talk on parenting, I am inevitably asked the question: 'Can you tell me how to get my child to do what I tell them to do?' The quest to find effective discipline techniques for children of all ages has a lot of followers. It's easy to recognise ineffective discipline: emotions out of control, impulsive slapping and exaggerated threats that will never be followed through.

The general wisdom on calm, effective parenting includes many familiar techniques for discipline such as time out, ignoring undesirable behaviour and removing privileges. Well-known techniques for reinforcing desirable behaviour include praise, granting extra privileges, and rewards such as presents and star charts. In many ways all of these approaches can be sound strategies that can bring about positive behaviour change in children and adolescents. But I wonder if you can see what is missing from all of them?

Behavioural approaches to parenting are all focused on influencing the conduct of the child rather than on the emotional regulation of the parent. While parenting our child is very different to managing our pets, I've been able to see some parenting principles illustrated as I watch how I operate with my one-year-old cocker spaniel puppy Hendrix. Food is a wonderful motivator for him to perform submissive behaviours by responding to commands such as 'sit', 'down', 'stay' and 'come'. I can even get Hendrix to drop his ball for me to throw, if I have a treat to give him. The problem is that he now has the idea that he is in charge of me as I hand food over to him and praise him for taking it. I realise that my focus on punishments and rewards is not helping me to earn his respect as the pack leader. The more useful approach with my puppy is for me to convey calm and strong leadership energy and refuse to move forward with an activity until the dog is in a submissive, non-aroused state. In this approach all the work is on myself as the owner and not directed at the dog. The dog senses when the owner is taking charge and not tolerating anxious, dominant behaviour.

Of course, our children are different to dogs in terms of their brain's capacity to process and remember, but we humans have more in common with other social mammals than we often like to think. My recent lessons with Hendrix are in line with what has been most helpful with my children. The grown-up approach of managing myself rather than using external motivators is harder work but the big-picture results, in terms of mature children, make it worth the effort.

In parenting, the biggest downside to relying on rewards and punishments is that our children learn to behave according to who's watching. This can leave them immaturely struggling to put in effort simply because it seems the right thing to do. The child or teen comes to look at their conduct in terms of what's in it for them or how they can avoid something unpleasant. Can you see how this doesn't take a child very far in developing an inner, thinking guidance system?

A parent who puts effort into clarifying their own values and doesn't waver from these in how they behave with their child, is likely to be more effective than one who relies on techniques directed at their children. This focus on the self of the parent rather than the child is conveyed through the language and action around the 'I': 'Here's where I stand on this issue and this is what I will do to back this up' rather than 'Here's what you should do and this is what will happen to you if you don't obey'.

Getting clearer about an 'I' position

The following are the key principles for holding an 'I' position. The parent:

» manages themself, not the child;

» doesn't try to control what's beyond their own choice to activate;

» doesn't expect words to achieve much and is willing to action what they say;

» doesn't crowd a child's developmental breathing space by pushing or pulling them into behaving as they desire.

The following are some examples of what might typically be said to a child by a parent, and how each might be replaced with a response that better reflects an 'I' position:

'You must stop doing that or I will send you to your room' might be replaced with:'I am going to have to go to another room because I can't concentrate on this task while there's so much noise.'

'If you stop that screaming now I will buy you a treat at the checkout' can be replaced with: 'I'm not going to keep shopping with all that fuss. If the screaming keeps up I will go straight home. I'll come back and do the shopping later instead of going to the park this afternoon.'

'I will give you extra pocket money if you do an hour of homework each night' is replaced with: 'I see it as your responsibility to satisfy the school's requirements, and I will not step in at the last minute if you haven't managed to get things done on time.'

'If you don't stop fighting with your brother I'm going to take away your PlayStation' is switched to :'I expect that you two need to learn how to play together cooperatively and I believe you can find a way to do it. If I come back in 5 minutes and you still haven't worked it out, I won't be willing to keep the computers on for the rest of the day.'

'How dare you swear at me? You're grounded!' can be replaced with: 'I'm not willing to be generous when I experience so much disrespect. I am pulling out from giving you that lift to your friend's house today.'

'Okay, I can see from your blank look that you aren't getting far with that homework and it's due tomorrow; let me help you out' is switched to: 'I'm hearing your complaints about this assignment. I'm willing to let you talk it through with me when I've finished my task, but I'm not willing to do any of the work for you.'

'Will you stop that whinging right now or I'll stop all our visits to the park this week!' is replaced with: no reaction from the parent, who continues to go about their own business.'

'Great job! That's the best drawing of a tree I've ever seen! You could be a great artist one day." Is switched to: 'I'm really interested in what you've created; I'd love to hear about your drawing.'

'You deserve a bravery award for changing your group of friends! I know you're going to be so much happier' is expressed more appropriately as: 'I think it's interesting to get to know new people. What do you think it will be like getting to know more of the others in your class?'

There is no magic in using the words of the 'I' position. The impact is not so much in the language but in the parent's inner conviction and their perseverance to continue to demonstrate this in action. When responding to a child's achievements, the parent expresses their genuine interest without trying to make the child feel a certain way. When the parent takes a stand about inappropriate behaviour, the child senses the difference of the parent's inner conviction and, after a time of testing, begins to manage themself better.

It takes some dedicated time to think things through for yourself, to know what your limits are and how you will live by them. Be prepared for your child to test out whether you really mean what you are saying you're willing and not willing to do. And be prepared to do, or not do, what you have stated. After a period of challenging your resolve, they will come to appreciate that they are dealing with an adult who is not having a knee-jerk reaction but is clear and trustworthy.

Adolescents confronting us with our immaturity

Keeping a focus on our thinking and behaviour as parents is especially difficult when parenting teenagers. Sometimes adolescent behaviours are full of so much impulsivity and intense emotion that we turn all our attention to trying to manage them. Many parents tell me that they wish they could fast forward the years that their children are thirteen through to eighteen. While it's easy to be derailed during our children's adolescence, this phase also provides some valuable practice opportunities for bringing our maturity up a notch.

Christine's effort to be more of a resource to her seventeen-year-old son Tom provides a good example. When I met with Christine, she was beside herself with worry about Tom. He had been staying up most nights sitting in front of his computer and was becoming increasingly moody and verbally aggressive with family members, especially his mum. Tom had grudgingly agreed to see his school counsellor in response to his mum's pressure, but Christine wanted to look at what she too could do to help her son. I asked her what had taken up most of her energies with Tom lately. Christine answered: 'My biggest worry has been Tom's school work. It was such a shock last year to see his report with his grades dropping so much. I've always believed that, of all my children, Tom was the bright one with great potential.'

I then asked Christine how she had responded to Tom's change in his results.

> I've been trying to motivate him and to get his study habits to an acceptable level. We have spent a lot of time together developing a study schedule that will help him to get back on track. I check in on him every now and then to see if he needs my help. I just know that his self-esteem will drop if his grades don't get back to what he is used to.

Christine and I explored together what aspects of her parenting were working and what strategies were not showing signs of helpfulness. She could see that not many of her helping efforts were actually assisting Tom or her relationship with him. With this awareness she set about getting back her clarity about her own responsibilities as Tom's mother. The following is a brief summary of the changes she made within herself in order to be a better resource to her son. Christine expressed to Tom:

I can see that it is not possible for me to make you do your work. How much work you put in is a decision that I see as entirely in your hands. I will be available to help you if you need it but I won't crowd your space. I certainly will not continue to allow the computer and Internet access to be on after I go to bed. I realise that if I don't step in and switch off our connection, I am a part of the problem of allowing computer time to come ahead of reasonable rest.

Christine stopped her practice of always supplying extra money for socialising and unlimited use of her car under all circumstances. She expressed that if she did not feel respected in terms of verbal attacks, she would not supply whatever he asked for. On the occasions when it was not convenient for her to let Tom use the car she would drive him to his friend's place and stop for a coffee together on the way.

It was extremely anxiety-provoking for Christine to step back from trying to direct Tom's study habits, as she was fearful that he would do no work and drop out of school as her younger brother had done. She stayed on track by reminding herself that the old approach was ineffective and seemed to be contributing to Tom's increasing agitation. She knew there were no guarantees that Tom would find his capacity to direct his work efforts but that if he was going to learn this for the future she had to stop intruding and trying to do it for him.

After a few months Christine reported some progress. Tom was less irritated and angry and had thanked his mother for getting off his back about school. His grades did not show much improvement, which was a challenge for Christine. She put a lot of work into calming her fears about Tom's future. To prevent her from cutting off around the school issues, Christine shared with Tom her experience of her brother dropping out of school and how she had realised this had added to her being a bit over the top about Tom's education. She tried to listen with respect and curiosity to his ideas about life after high school without pushing her advice onto him. She was surprised that occasionally Tom would actually ask for her opinion on courses he was interested in.

Christine also turned her attention to her marriage and realised how much she had accommodated her husband, with him becoming increasingly devoted to work while she devoted herself to their children. She started to share with him how hard she was finding the challenges of parenting teenagers. Previously she had focused on telling him what he should say to Tom to address her worries. Christine also allowed her husband much more uninterrupted time with Tom. Previously she had been quick to jump into their relationship to smooth things over whenever she felt that her husband was not handling things sensitively enough.

Pulling it together

Children will have a smoother growing-up trajectory when they have a parent who focuses on being a principled individual. It isn't the goal that both parents become clones of each other, always trying to appear to be on the same page with their child. The reality is that both parents are different individuals and will have varied styles of operating as parents. This helps prepare children for life where adapting to different styles of teachers, and later employees, contributes to their healthy adjustment as adults. So this means that a parent can take the focus off trying to correct or co-opt support from their parenting partner, as well as trying to direct the child, and simply make a project out of maturing themself.

The following checklist is a summary of what's involved when parents attend to themselves and give their children breathing space to manage their own growing-up challenges. Remember that it's an ideal we are unlikely to fully reach, but it can help us to know that our efforts are heading in the direction of maturity. And these efforts contribute to a more mature cycle of reactions in the parent–child relationship.

» Decision-making about what the child needs is not driven by the feelings of the moment but by thoughtfully acquired principles.

» Both parents willingly share their thinking about parenting and listen carefully to the other. Neither assumes that they know best. Each lives by the principle that they are responsible for thinking things through for themselves.

» Each parent can talk to the other about his or her anxieties about being adequate parents but they do not expect the other to relieve these for them. Each is a listening resource to the other without feeling compelled to take responsibility for the other.

» Each parent can relate to the child from a place of self-awareness and without unfounded fears about the child's wellbeing. Hence they are positive about the child without anxiously perceiving the child as needing special attention and praise.

» Both parents enjoy discussing their child and experience

pleasure in watching the child develop. However, neither is preoccupied with the child and each can find time for themselves and their marriage.

» Parents are clear about the limits of what they will do for their child.

» Each parent is comfortable allowing the other to manage his or her relationship with the child. They are not drawn into intervening to take over from the other parent or criticising the parenting of the other.

» Each parent takes responsibility for their own efforts to be a principled parent and doesn't look to the other parent to fill in their confidence gaps.

» Each parent attends to the tensions in their marriage by expressing their ideas without blame. They know that working on any stuck points in their marriage is the most useful thing they can do to not confuse their parenting.

The mature parent, who is reliably present for their child and speaks with conviction about what they will or will not do, doesn't give their child scope for lots of emotional reaction. It's fascinating to see how predictably a child will listen to a parent speaking a thoughtful 'I will not' message, as predictably as the child will not listen to an anxious 'you will not' message.

Have you noticed this difference in the attentiveness of children and adolescents to a parent or teacher? Do you recognise that glazed-over look in the face of a thirteen-year-old as their parent lectures them about what they must do? Very often you can see a child respond to pushing and pulling with a counter-reaction or a half-hearted compliance. What a contrast to observe a child tune into an adult who is being clear about what they will not do. This child, who sees their parent's certainty in the position they take, is left to consider their own responsibility. Herein lies the key to how grown-up parents facilitate grown-up children.

Questions for reflection

» Do I put more energy into managing myself as a responsible parent or trying to shape my children?

» Do I know what I am and am not willing to do when one of my children behaves irresponsibly? How much of my parenting is couched in 'you' messages compared with 'I' messages?

» What issues have I avoided addressing with my spouse and have replaced with attention onto one or more of my children? Is my conversation with my spouse more about us or more about our children?

Extra Resources for Building Confident Parents

1. Healthy child & adolescent development

Connection and autonomy in balance encourages maturation.
Maturity grows as connection with caregivers gradually allows more independence. From birth through to adulthood a key developmental task for a child is to gradually reduce their dependence on their mother, on both parents, and on other adults, and increase their capacity to manage upsets, new challenges, and ways to socialise. Early opportunities to experience the stress of short separations from caregivers, is the start of the child growing some autonomy. The key to assisting a child to develop their resilience in growing more in independence is to provide balanced connection and autonomy experiences appropriate to their age. Connection shows interest and support while always treating the child as a separate person who is learning to manage their own life tasks. Allowing even a young child opportunities to explore their world independently from the caregiver is an important way to support healthy development. At all stages of parent-child development, an equal balance of connection and opportunity for independence is optimal.

Milestones for managing emotions: self-regulation
Managing strong impulses and feelings is an important developmental task. The child needs lots of practice to manage without others taking over this task. The development of self-regulation is central to successful adaptation in childhood and

adolescence. Self-regulation has been defined as biological processes that serve to manage:

Fear: reactivity and fear responses

Social Extremes: exaggerated social withdrawal or extroversion

Irresponsible Behaviour: the effortful control of behaviour

Self-regulatory capacity increases across most developmental periods of childhood and continues well into adolescence and early adulthood. It can be worked on and improved throughout life. A parent who works to practice calming their intense emotions contributes to an environment that fosters the child's self-regulation.

The developing brain

Experiences with the world and relationships have a major impact on which neural connections are established, reinforced, and maintained and which connections are pruned. This is good news! The brain has great plasticity which means that repeated new relationship interactions can gradually wire new neural pathways. Rushing a child, overcrowding or interrupting their problem-solving process is disruptive to their thinking brain development.

Impulse control & mental flexibility reach adult levels by age 12 and abstract thinking and problem-solving abilities have a gradual progression from primary school age into high school. At 12 years, children have an increased ability to monitor and flexibly alter their behaviour according to changing demands in their environment.

Adolescence

During adolescence, the brain undergoes significant maturation, particularly in the frontal lobes. While the adolescent brain is fast approaching full maturation there are still under-developed pathways between the frontal lobes and the part of the brain that deals with relationships (parietal lobe) and emotional impulses (amygdala). Hence they still require some supportive assistance with decision-making and some guidance and limits in areas where impulsive behaviours can be harmful to self and others. A wise parent, who can set some parameters, is important as long as they are not excessively protective or restrictive.

Self-regulation in the parent encourages self-regulation in the child/adolescent

When a parent can be calmer a child learns to calm themselves down more effectively. When stress levels are high, both the child and the adult brain is overly directed by the lower brain instincts and reactions. There are more pathways going up from the lower brain than those coming down from the complex problem-solving frontal lobes. A parent can't be in control of how the child's brain functions, but they can make progress to control their own reactions to stress. A parent who doesn't allow their lower brain emotional impulses to run the show contributes to a less reactive and more thoughtful child/adolescent. This is a resource for the child's improved self-regulation.

» What kind of parent connection do you think supports a child's development of self-regulation (managing fear, social extremes and irresponsible behaviours)?

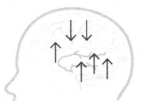

The Changeable brain

An anxious brain is a 'bottom up' brain. A thoughtful brain is a 'top down' brain that has more messages coming from the top frontal lobes (neo cortex).

2. The Parenting Worry Cycle

What happens with an increase in worry focus directed towards a child/adolescent? See if you can follow this common cycle for conscientious, caring parents:

» In response to a parent's concerned attentions, the child becomes attuned to being nervously monitored and reacts with increasing self-consciousness.

» The child's anxious response can be in the form of increased neediness/dependence or agitated/rebellious behaviour. A stirred-up child usually increases their impulsive and demanding behaviour, while a needy child increases their childlikeness and dependence.

» The parents in turn may inadvertently increase their focus on fixing things for the child by either increasing their corrections or their support. In this concern-driven cycle, the parent partly gives up being a separate person from the child and the child grows up borrowing some of their self from the reactions they elicit from their parent.

» The stirred-up child is restricted in their capacity to find ways to calm themself and contain their impulsiveness; and the needy child is compromised in learning to manage their own worries.

Reflect on this example of a worry cycle. How is this similar

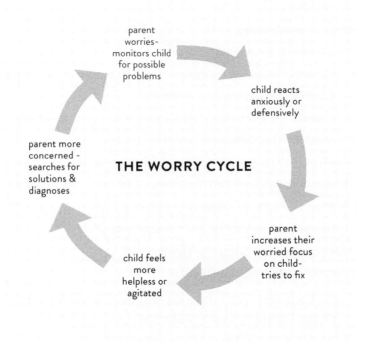

3. Parent self-regulation promotes child's resilience

Experiments with parent self-regulation = a key to building resilience.

What is resilience?

For the child/adolescent:

» Distress tolerance: tolerating one's own and others' uncomfortable emotions/distress

» Calming self: capacity to calm down stress arousal and intense emotions using inner resources

» Problem-solving effort: capacity to come up with logical solutions to one's own problems (not the other's problem)

» Aware of self and others: ability to focus on and describe (speak for) self, more than reacting to others

How can parents promote this?

By working on parent resilience:

» Parent distress tolerance: tolerating one's own and others' uncomfortable emotions/ distress

» Parent calming self: capacity to calm down stress arousal and intense emotions using inner resources

» Parent problem-solving effort: capacity to come up with logical solutions to one's own problems (not the other's problem)

» Parent aware of self and others: ability to focus on and

describe (speak for) self, more than reacting to others

What to observe:
Everyone gets anxious. Often anxiety triggers are outside of our awareness and our brain has learned instinctively to relieve the experience of heightened tension. The more a parent can bring their anxiety triggers and patterned ways of relieving tension into their awareness, the more they are able to bring leadership in emotional tone into the family.

The presence of just one less anxious adult can reduce the intensity level of the whole system. We can reduce or contain our anxiety by drawing on our internal resources or by being distracted by external things. The more we can use our own resources to contain anxiety, the less likely our tensions spread unhelpfully to others.

» What can you observe in yourself that tells you your tensions/worry levels are increasing?

» What do you notice in your body? Your breathing, heart rate, stomach tension, fingertip temperature, muscle tensions?

» What do you notice about your thinking patterns when tensions mount? (negative thinking; blaming of self or others; fear of the future; fear of repeating the past; fear of something bad happening; excessive concern over one part of your life, such as cleanliness.)

» What do you notice about your relationship patterns when tensions mount? Who do you focus on most? Who do you withdraw from/avoid?

» What do you notice about your behaviours when tension

mounts? What are your distracters? How does your eating, exercising, drinking, use of medication, shopping, working etc. change when tension is higher?

Can you notice using any of your own resources to manage?

» Using relaxation techniques? Ways to reduce your body's tension signs.

» Using your logic? Is this degree of worry in proportion to exactly what is going on now?

» Using your principles? What principles for the kind of person/parent I wish to be can keep me in balance right now? (E.g. I am committed to not attacking others; to behaving with integrity; to being honest and direct.)

The anxiety of progress:
Often changing from external distracters to using our own resources leaves us feeling more anxious and destabilized for a time. This is to be expected as any change from habit is uncomfortable. It's helpful to remember that this kind of change tension is about making progress. It doesn't feel comfortable but we know that it is aimed at being more constructive.

Backwards tension/anxiety	progress tension/anxiety
Avoid what is uncomfortable	Tolerate what is uncomfortable

4. Positive connection: focus on capabilities and maturity, not on symptoms.

The key principles for talking with your child about their challenges in ways that don't reinforce dependency:

There is growing research showing that parents who are connected with their child/ young person, without being overly involved, can assist the young person to grow in resilience. It is especially challenging to hold back from intervening with anxious or struggling children and child/adolescents. Seeing them grapple with their distress and struggle to find their own way through bad feelings is hard to watch, but in the bigger picture of their development, skills learned from within the child/young person, rather than loaned by the parent, are more helpful in building a their own skills and confidence.

Jumping in to fix things for the child can bring short-term relief – but longer-term, the young person's development of their own self-regulation and problem solving gets held back. Holding back from fixing, taking over, reassuring and instructing will be very uncomfortable in the short-term but creates space for the young person to develop their own capacities to cope with stress for the long-term.

The key principles are:

»   Parent to be present and attentive but not crowding their child/adolescent. (Learning to be quiet = watch, wait, be curious).

»   Parent to be genuinely interested without taking over

through directing, problem solving, criticizing or over-praising.

» Parent to ask questions about the young person's ideas for dealing with the situation and listen well.

» Parent may share advice only when the young person has worked to think through their own ideas.

» The parent shares their thinking rather than tells the child what they should do. They might share how they manage similar situations as a way of providing guidance rather than thinking for their child.

Think about how much of your interaction time with your child/adolescent is around problems and symptoms.

Notice when your interaction is caught up with:

» Monitoring

» Criticizing

» Instructing or commanding

» or "Doing for".

How much does connection happen at calm times when the child/adolescent is engaged in a positive activity?

What opportunities can you find to practice:

» Coming alongside, noticing

» Practicing interested silence

» Reflecting

» Acknowledging (different to strong praising) e.g. "I can see how much you persevered to achieve such a good result" rather than "You are fantastic!"

5. Parent job description & leadership

What do you think about these contrasting job descriptions for you as a parent?

ANXIOUSLY FOCUSED ON THE CHILD	vs.	MATURELY FOCUSED ON PARENT JOB DESCRIPTION
To resolve my child's distress		To tolerate my child's upset sufficiently for my child to learn to manage their emotions
To solve my child's problems		To invite my child's problem-solving
To direct my child's thinking		To be engaged with my child's thinking and then share some of my thinking
To push my child to do what I want		To only do what I am in control of and what supports my values
To pull my child away from risk		To set up boundaries and allow my child room to make mistakes
To make my child confident, happy, successful, popular		To be a consistent, caring, principled, respectful, interested, loving parent
To make my child my project		To live a principled life that is an example to my child

Am I becoming a parent leader? Characteristics of a family leader – Dr. Murray Bowen

This is a person who comes to understand better his or her part in the relationship system problem and is willing to do something about it. They give up hoping others will change, not out of anger or guilt, but out of the conviction that they are part of the problem and thus part of the solution.

A family leader:

» Possesses the courage to define self

» Is invested in the welfare of the family at least as much as in his/her own welfare

» Is neither angry nor dogmatic

» Directs energy to changing self rather than telling others what they should do.

Which of these qualities are in line with your goals as a parent?

* Resources 1-5 from the Parent Hope Project—A manualised Program for restoring parent's hope in their capacity to assist their struggling child.

6. *Becoming a more mature helper [parent]*

Excerpt from Ch 16 Jenny Brown Growing Yourself Up (2nd Ed, 2017) – The Grown-Up Helper

> In part, parenting is a helping process. Hence it relevant to include these thoughts about the kind of help that facilitates resilience rather than dependence. It is also useful for parents to consider how they can be central to assisting their child through difficult times by adjusting the way they interact with their child. A confident parent works on themselves before rushing to find a professional service to treat their child. If professional supports are utilised the parent doesn't distance themselves but is willing to work on discovering how they can be a resource for their child's restored resilience.

The list below is a brief summary for any who want to lend a hand to others in their own growing up journey. It starts with identifying the kind of helping process that isn't helpful, before reviewing what a mature helping process involves. You may wish to use it to identify your own helping pitfalls as well as your strengths.

What kind of help doesn't help?

» Help that takes on another's functioning and responsibility.

» Help that quickly gives advice — telling others what to do.

» Help that just diagnoses and prescribes the way to treat.

» Help that takes sides/agrees that other people are the problem and need to change.

» Help that tries to remove the other's distress.

And for the helping avoiders:

» Helping by always staying out of the way. Avoiding saying the wrong thing, making things more upsetting. Leaving the role to others.

What kind of help helps?

» Help that comes alongside the other and allows them to be in distress.

» Help that gives room for the other to find their best way through.

» Help that listens well, that asks questions about how the person is dealing with their difficulty. The helper shares ideas that are raised in the conversation but refrains from directing.

» Help that sees that many people contribute to symptoms in individuals and relationships. Rather than taking sides, a helper is interested in assisting the other in discovering what part they play in the problem patterns.

» Help that broadens a person's thinking about themselves in their relationships rather than a narrow focus on individual diagnosis.

And for the helping avoiders:

» Help by being present, making time to be in good contact with a person during their time of struggle. Setting aside one's own discomfort about the other's situation and emotions to be ready to listen and to be a friend.

7. What to look for from a helping professional

If you are in a professional therapy relationship or looking for an effective counsellor/therapist you may be rethinking the nature of the helping process you, or your child, are a part of. When considering what kind of help assists people to regain their own confidence it is worth asking yourself the following questions about your helping relationship:

» Am I asked questions that get me thinking of new ways to understand and resolve my difficulty? Or are my viewpoints all accepted?

» Am I respected and listened to as a competent person? Or am I being pitied or overly protected?

» Am I given suggestions that build upon the description and ideas I have come up with myself? Or am I given lots of advice?

» Am I encouraged to consider my part, and the way each person affects each other? Or is my view of the problem in others affirmed and agreed with? -

» Do I leave my sessions thinking about my own pain in the context of relationship patterns? Or am I left thinking about how hard done-by I am?

***

Effective helping is not that different to maturity in any relationship role? The effort is to stay within one's own parameters and not do for others what they will, in the longer term, be better off learning to do for themselves.

Above all, it requires the helper to attend to observing and managing themselves as much as listening to and attending to the one who is being helped.

* Resources 6-7 from the book, Growing Yourself Up: How to bring your best to all of life's relationships by Dr Jenny Brown.

References

Introduction:
1. Brown, J. 2008, We Don't Need Your Help but Will You Please Fix Our Children. *Australian and New Zealand Journal of Family Therapy*, 29, 2
2. Bowen, M. 1978, *Family Therapy in Clinical practice*. New York: Aronson.
3. Brown, J. 2017, Growing Yourself Up: How to bring your best to all of life's relationships. Wollombi, Exisle Publishing.

Mini Book:
1. Gilbert, R. 1999, *Connecting with Our Children: Guiding principles for parents in a troubled world*, John Wiley, New York, p.11.
2. Stearns, P.N. 2003, Anxious Parents: A history of modern childrearing in America, New York University Press, New York.

Extra resource pages from:
1. The Parent Hope Project & Parent Confidence Project Manuals: www.parenthopeproject.com.au

Further Resources

- **For parents:** Discover the **Confident Parenting Seminar Series** and more at www.parentproject.com.au

- **For family health professionals – manualised programs** The Parent Hope Project & The Parent Confidence Project: www.parenthopeproject.com.au

- **Growing Yourself Up: How to bring your best to all of life's relationships by Dr Jenny Brown (available at all book outlests):** https://exislepublishing.com/product/growing-2nd-edition

- **The Family Systems Institute Sydney:** www.thefsi.com.au

- **The Bowen Center for the Study of the Family, Washington DC:** www.thebowencenter.org

Printed in Australia
AUHW011421260520
328333AU00007B/7

9 780648 578529